The Best Advice I Ever Gave

The Best Advice
I Ever Gave

94 essential tips for making
your dreams come true

BARBARA SHER

Beyond Mountains

Table of Contents

Introduction

Hi, Dear Reader, Dreamer, Genius.

Let me tell you why I gathered this group of bite-size lessons together for you to read. I've been counselling for many years, helping people discover what they really want to do with their lives, and coming up with ways for them to do it. That's my mission and I'm dead serious about it.

Through all that time I found that some of the things I said in sessions or in my books or at my workshops, things I'd learned from experience, were unusually important to people. How do I know that? I'd hear from them, often years later, often in emails or Christmas cards, and they'd tell wonderful stories about what they had accomplished, and almost invariably they'd thank me for some one thing I said - "I never forgot what you told me. It changed my thinking" or "That one thing you said changed the way I did so many things" or "I can't forget something you said. It changed the way I saw myself."

If short bits of advice can make that much difference, it's important to get them out to as many of you as possible. So for the last few years I've gathered together the ones people mentioned most often, and I'm putting them into this book

Now, 94 might look like a lot of tips, but I think every tip in this book will be important to you sooner or later. Since no-one can predict which of these tips will make the doors swing open for you and give you the best chance to achieve your dreams, I've included all the essential ones.

I think you'll find that this book will be a kind of friend when you need one. A buddy who's there when things get tough, who believes in you, who will remind you who you are and what you need when everything conspires to make you forget.

You see, you were put here to do something extraordinary. Something no-one else can do. Maybe you don't know that, or maybe you don't always remember, but I can never forget it. You're one of a kind – a new creature on this planet who sees everything in a new way. That means your dreams are new too. And that means you can't always get the understanding you need to develop your own vision. Precious talent can go wasted ot unused because you didn't get that understanding. I can't stand that.

So often we listen to the words of critics - even well-wishers - who don't have any idea who we are or what we're talking about. And what they say makes us lose confidence in our own dreams. We back down - not for a good reason, (although boy! do we come up with reasons!) but just because no-one was around who understood what we were talking about.

Some of these reasons we give are excuses because we're afraid, like "I can't just do whatever I want - I have responsibilities" or "I'll get rich first, then I can go after my dreams" or "I'd have to quit my job and go back to school for years". They look real, but they're not.

Do you know how to tell the difference between a valid reason and an excuse? Pay attention and you'll see that excuses give you a sense of relief. But real obstacles give you a feeling of disappointment. That's the kind of thing you have to know when you go after a dream, so you won't trick yourself into stopping.

Some of the reasons we give are simple mistakes. We make assumptions that aren't true, like "You can't go to medical school at your age", or "No-one will hire you to do the things you love", or "It costs too much money to travel and see the world". Mistaken assumptions are treacherous because they're invisible. When you assume something is true, you never think to investigate it.

So how are you supposed to find it? In this collection of tips I'm going to teach you how to send out a search and destroy mission for hidden assumptions that works every time. So that's what this collection of tips is all about.

I'm hoping that reading these tips and getting this advice that has stood the test of time will end the tricks isolation plays on us and bring all your dreams to life. Now that would make me feel like a million bucks.

You are going to be terrific!

Tip 1: Forget your skills set and your core competencies

Yes, that's what I said! Ignore your resume, too. Those are all good for getting a job to tide you over, but they're irrelevant for finding out what you're brilliant at. Don't go looking for your dream job in the want ads or on a list of careers because it's not there.

What if your vocational testing results say that you would make a great warden in a maximum-security prison, and the notion does not thrill you? Then ignore the test! Skills aren't the same as gifts. You may have had no opportunity to develop your gifts at all, but they're gifts just the same.

Face it: we're all good at something we don't like. Maybe that's playing piano or trimming hedges or cleaning up a mess, but if it doesn't make you happy, don't be fooled into trying to build a life around that skill.

When I ask people what they'd enjoy doing they often say, "Well, I could be a bookkeeper ..." and then I have to stop them. I say, "I didn't ask what you *could* do, I asked what you enjoy doing." Start asking yourself that question and you'll start tracking down what you love.

PS: If you're thinking, "What good does it do to find what I love? I have to earn some money!" don't worry about it. In these tips you're going to learn how to do both. Read on!

Tip 2: Forget other people's dreams of great wealth

When you follow someone else's dreams, you risk losing sight of what you love – and the most blinding dream is the dream of wealth.

"I focused on becoming wealthy for so long I have no idea what I really want," said a man at one of my workshops. Too many people fall for the glitter of wealth without realizing that they may not need a huge amount of money at all. Focusing on wealth can eat up all your time, and all your creative energy as well.

The truth is, deep down not everyone really wants a million dollars. The fantasy of wealth is just a shiny piece of magic that promises we can have any dream at all. In our culture, and most cultures, money is highly valued, and few people will belittle or criticize you for going after it. But dreams are as individual as people, and they're not easy for others to understand. That's why we often get pushed to choose what others value.

When you're the culprit – when the only one pushing you toward dreams of your family or friends or culture is you

– stop and think for a moment. Maybe you're just dodging the complex and scary issues of discovering who you are, and what you'd really love to do with your life.

The price for going after other people's dreams is high. In the rush for success and security our real dreams get lost. That's like losing your compass in the wilderness, because dreams aren't silly, childish things. We don't invent our dreams. We don't even choose them. They're urgent telegrams sent by our biology and our personal history. Simply put: an eagle locked in a cage dreams of flying and nothing else. If you ignore your dream for too long, you'll start to feel despair – and no amount of wealth will cure that.

Tip 3: Find your own dreams

Think you don't know what they are? Well, you do. Everyone does. Why can't you see them? Because you think they're impossible and that makes them invisible. The truth is, until you get started you don't know what's possible. You're going to find that out as you go along, but first things first.

Your dreams are based on your gifts. Nature wants you to use the talents inside you. Individual talent obviously helps our species survive, and using talent *feels* good. It makes you happy. So to find what you love, simply use the same technique you use every day to decide what you want to eat: think of pizza and wait for a response from inside. If nothing comes, think of another kind of food and continue, until that response pops up and says, "Yummy!"

To find your dreams just think of anything you've ever enjoyed, or anything you've heard of that sounded interesting – say, "joining the circus." While you're imagining it, check yourself for levels of happiness (I call them "H-Levels"). On a scale of one to ten, if one is just boring and ten is pure heaven, what number would you assign to joining the circus?

If you pull anything below a 4, you can cross it off and forget it. If you get a 7 or above, pay attention. If it's anything in the middle forget it. You'll waste too much time thinking about it. But if it's above a 7, write it down and go on to the next fantasy. Listening to your H-Levels is good practice, and you just might stumble on that dream right here at the beginning of the book!

Tip 4: Forget the rules; whoever made them didn't have you in mind

Of course, you've had to follow a bunch of rules to get this far (paying your rent and looking both ways before you cross the street are good ones to hang on to). But going after your dreams will take you into new, unexplored territory with new rules. It's no use bringing along the old ones because they might not apply here.

"Tough-it-out" rules, like "a quitter never wins" may have been useful when you were playing team sports in school, but they won't be much help to you now. When I started searching for what I'd really love to do, I first went through every rule I'd learned about being in a positive mood, concentrating on my skills, increasing my willpower, raising my self esteem, etc. And I dumped them one by one, because they just didn't work for me. To get your dream, you're going to have to create a new set of rules, ones that work for you.

Here's a good way to know if a rule works for you: imagine doing what you love – really try to put yourself there – and then see yourself saying that rule. Does it make sense in the context of your dream? Does it help you to do your best, or does it ring strange somehow?

If you'd love to ride horses, which rule works better for you: "A quitter never wins" or "Stay in the moment"?

Tip 5: Don't worry about money just yet

I've talked about wealth already, but this is different. I'm talking now about all those thoughts you're having – here at the beginning – of how you're going to earn a living. The fastest way to destroy the exploration of your gifts and talents is to get too practical too soon. Just about everyone who comes to see me automatically buries every wonderful discovery of their talent within moments by saying, "But you can't make money doing that."

This is what I tell them:

You can earn a living doing anything. (Whether or not you want to is another matter.) But it's not time to think about money yet. Finding what you love – by listening for those Happiness Levels inside you – needs all your attention. For now, pretend you're rich and don't need to earn any money at all. When your dream starts to show itself, you'll see just how many ways there are to do it, both for money and for love.

Tip 6: Don't waste your time thinking about why you want something

Who cares why? We spend far too much time analyzing our reasons for wanting what we do: ("I guess I want to perform because I always needed attention as a kid. I was such a showoff.") That kind of analysis and self-criticism is the first step to dropping a dream. And then you'll start doubting your right to dream at all. I say, who cares why you want it? If it feels good, you've touched a talent or a need. Go after it. It's trying to tell you something.

What if it's not the right dream? Well, that's always better than being stuck. And even if this idea turns out to be a mistake, you've got to take it on anyway. You won't be able to move forward until you get it out of your system. That's all part of your education. You're the navigator: you can correct your path whenever you need to.

But most important is that you've got to get into action. This is not a blank check for being reckless. Even if you're sure of what you want, you should always start out by putting your toe in the water instead of jumping. Try things out in a small, safe way to begin with. Be sure not to burn any bridges or use up all your resources – you might need them later if you change your mind – but do go after that dream.

Someone years ago sent me this bit of wisdom in a letter: "Having your dreams fulfilled can be more therapeutic than having them analyzed." I like that, don't you?

Tip 7: Don't crush your dreams with "conventional wisdom"

Most mistaken assumptions are based on conventional wisdom – and some of them call for special mention. Here are the dreamkillers I hear most often:

"You need credentials."

"If it was easy, everybody would be doing it."

"Who'll hire you for that!"

Conventional wisdom just betrays a huge lack of imagination and information. Closer investigation usually proves it wrong. The truth is, you often don't *need* credentials. What's easy for you isn't easy for everyone, and people today are being hired for thinking "outside of the box," not following convention. But more to the point, who said you had to be hired by anyone to do what you love? Who says you can't do it on your own?

Here's a great way to deal with those and all other dream smashers. Instead of taking them at face value, turn them into questions (see Tip 58). Do you really need credentials to do what you love? Is it really too hard for you to do? And who just might hire people to do it? (Or even better, as I said, is there some way you could do it on your own?)

Then go out there and get the answers

Tip 8: Forget power fantasies: go looking for strategies

The bookshelves and late-night TV screens are filled with people trying to show you that you have no limitations, you are all-powerful, and you can't be beat if only you believe it. These techniques are based on male combat and competition models, and they've often proved useful for the very short-term challenge – one skirmish, one football game. Unfortunately, they're almost useless when it comes to dream searching.

Two problems have emerged. The worst is the growing numbers of people who have given up on themselves because they can't succeed at believing they are all-powerful gods. The second is that people are forgetting what is *really* required to create confidence: things like support and strategic thinking.

Pretending to yourself that you have the power of a god might help you with immediate superhuman feats, like running the 4-minute mile or lifting a car off your neighbor (although it might not). But finding and achieving a dream requires more than a burst of speed or power.

You don't need muscle – you need a plan. Pretending you're a giant can mean you fear that you're really tiny – and that's not true either. So relax and join the human race. Then you can make room for some real-world, human-sized thinking. Humans have very good brains, and our greatest strength is the ability to develop excellent strategies.

Tip 9: Forget what you "should" love

Sometimes you get the feeling you should love art or theatre or business, because everybody expects you to. Or because it's such an obviously good choice for the superior person or for a "winner". Or because that's what the smartest or most successful or most interesting people seem to love.

But nobody really knows what anybody else "should" love. You can't *choose* what you love; you can only discover it. Following anything but your heart will lead you down long pathways that will use up a lot of your time and creativity needlessly. And you'll have to retrace your tracks eventually if you ever want to be happy and productive.

Search for what you *do* love, no matter where it takes you. When you find it, you can decide how you want to bring it into your life: as a hobby, a passion, a career, an income stream or a business.

That's the only way to find out what you *should* love. If you do it that way, you'll know for sure it's right.

Tip 10: Forget what people might think

We often put our dreams aside for fear of what the world will think of us. If we experienced criticism growing up, we learn to be very careful not to stand out or draw attention to ourselves. But think about it: what's the worst thing that can happen? The world will think you're foolish? I promise you, it's worth it. If they smile at your attempts, smile right back at them.

What's the best that can happen? Look at anyone who's going after what they love, regardless of the opinion of others. That kind of happiness is wonderful to see. Once you let yourself focus on what you're doing instead of what others might be thinking, you'll experience the same kind of happiness and you'll never go back. (You might find that the hecklers start asking you for advice on how to follow *their* dreams.) We can all learn something from the person who wrote this letter:

"Dear Barbara,

On this, my 54th birthday, I've decided to dedicate the coming year to learning how to live my life the way I really want to. Every day I'm going to remind myself to do what matters to me no matter what anybody will think. And especially to do it no matter what I <u>assume</u> other people will think."

Tip 11: Don't be desperate; you're not really in a hurry

"I've *got* to find out what I want, the time is passing so fast, I feel panicky!" I hear this all the time. Nine times out of ten, the person speaking is around 27 years old. But even if you're older, don't trust that panic. Take a deep breath, heave a sigh, and continue working toward your dream, with patience.

If hurrying would speed up the process, I'd tell you to do it; but it does exactly the opposite. When you're spinning your wheels you can't see, hear, taste, touch or smell. You wouldn't know what you wanted if it flew into your pocket. That kind of panic is usually a mild form of hysteria that covers up sorrow.

The fear of pain is something all of us carry inside, but the moment you let yourself experience that feeling, the sadness, by just heaving a few sighs, or maybe even letting a tear flow – the fear actually disappears and the sadness turns out not to be monumental at all. Your anxiety will melt away long enough for you to do some real, constructive thinking.

Tip 12: Forget what you used to think you'd love

If you wanted to be a movie star or a fireman as a kid, chances are you outgrew that dream without much soul-searching. (If you didn't, you must pursue it!) But sometimes your early dreams of what you love aren't so easily understood or outgrown, even when they should be.

Helen, a client of mine, had always dreamed of being a writer, perhaps an investigative newspaper reporter. Finally, after saving some money, she quit her job as a secretary so she could go to work for a small newspaper. To her shock, she didn't enjoy writing after all. She was appalled. All those years she'd dreamed of writing and now she didn't really like it! Helen felt foolish and didn't know what to do next.

Was this a disaster? Not at all. Crossing an old dream off your list clears the path for you to find a new one. Helen was now free to look for a dream that really mattered to her. But before she discarded this old dream and picked up a new one, I thought it was important for her to understand how the mistake was made. We didn't want her to accidentally give up some part of that dream that was still essential to her. So Helen took a careful look at why she had ever imagined she would like writing in the first place.

"In high school I wrote an opinion column for the school paper," she told me, "and got respected and listened to. I loved it. I assumed writing for a newspaper was the way to continue my happy path. But it wasn't any fun at all because I never got to say what I wanted. So after that I took classes in novel writing and then non-fiction writing, where I had complete control over what I said, but that wasn't fun either. That's when I came to see you."

Together we isolated the elements in Helen's first writing experience in high school that had been so exciting and satisfying, and we found they had very little to do with writing itself. Helen needed to be listened to for her knowledge and opinions, to be heard and respected, to do good in the world.

It was a revelation. Instead of merely walking away from writing, Helen took these essential elements as guidelines for a different career. She found it at her local community college. Today Helen gives literacy classes to adults, and loves every minute of it. "I can see the difference I'm making", she told me, "and I can see the respect and appreciation in everyone's eyes. This work is perfect for me."

So examine anything you once loved, and check it closely to see if you still love it. If not, find the elements that still appeal to you and save them for your future searches, and then cross that outdated dream off the list. Don't waste another minute on it. Now, you're free to get started on the crucial search for what you really *do* love.

Tip 13: Dump your expectations

Learn to welcome the unexpected. It will give you opportunities and experiences and information you'd never have thought to ask for. The possibilities that await you in this world are much larger than your personal knowledge of it, and better things can happen than you were able to imagine. Keep your mind open, and don't discount the oddball finding, the unexpected door that opens. Look at this letter I got:

"Dear Barbara

I read all your books and what stuck in my mind was that you have to do what you love! I didn't follow it at first, but then last month I went on an Internet auction and found myself sneaking looks at antique dolls for sale.

Understand, I'm a businesswoman and have supported my family for years. I can hardly remember having dolls as a child. I felt that such silly, girlish stuff was off limits for me. But I ordered about 10 inexpensive, rather worn-looking dolls, and when they arrived in the mail I realized I was in love with them! I love dolls. How astounding!

I've decided to go after that dream, no matter where it takes me, and it's taking me in some wonderful directions. For one thing, I've discovered there are no doll museums in my city and I've begun a search to gather women with their own antique doll collections together, to perhaps start one. I haven't been this excited about anything in years."

Tip 14: Never forget you're an original

"What if I'm *not* an original?" you might think. Well, put it out of your mind. Even if you wanted to copy someone else, you'd still slip up and do it your own way. In any case, it's not your job to try to be original, and it's impossible to be anything else.

Visit a drawing class sometime to remind yourself. Just look at the difference in each student's drawing of the same still life and you'll understand how differently each of us sees the same thing. Don't worry about originality. It is your happy, inevitable destiny to be an original. Just do the work you love most and do it with all your heart.

The finished product will seem very normal to you, and very original to everyone else. That's the way it's supposed to be.

Tip 15: Don't rank worldly success above happiness

And don't assume they're the same thing. We often get mesmerized by the gleam of fame, wealth, power, and the admiration of others, before we get to know who we really are.

Some people's natures are completely suited to such dreams, but many others find themselves swept along by the current into lives that don't suit them at all. When they realize they'd be happier pursuing something besides wealth, often they get no confirmation from those around them.

If you're one of these people, it's time to do your own thinking. It's not necessary to jump ship and move to a desert island. You could change your mind and then you'd need the airfare to get out of there. But it is necessary to realize that your happiness counts, and then find ways to carefully back out of the bad contract you made when you were too young to know better. Think about it!

Tip 16: Don't habitually put loved ones' dreams before yours

Helping your family and your friends realize their dreams probably makes you feel wonderful. Putting yourself last might not bother you at all. You might never feel tired or unappreciated either. But there's one thing I bet you've overlooked. It might make them feel good to help you achieve your dreams too. It's amazing how rarely that occurs to us. And if they can't give you help for some reason (like they're only 4 years old) wake up to the fact that it would make them feel good to see you spend some time happily working on your own dreams.

To be the only gift-giver is a form of selfishness. Don't hoard all the generosity! Share it by putting yourself right up there at the top of your list of people whose dreams you care about. Give it a try!

Tip 17: Make friends with the Internet

Isolation is the dreamkiller because it allows ignorance to flourish. The Internet is an information miracle. In your home, at 3 a.m., with no inside connections, you can find out almost anything you need to know in minutes.

Learning to check things out on the Internet as a first action will change your life in a profound way. Over and over you'll see real information replace a dead-end with new opportunity. You can find people to help you, too – exactly the kind of people you need in your search. And the nature of the Internet is that anonymous people are happy to share information. There's no information more up to date, no group of people more willing to share their information and experience, and therefore almost no better way to get rid of outdated ideas than heading for the World Wide Web.

If I'm preaching to the converted, jump to the next tip. If not, don't waste another minute proudly scorning the new technology (or being afraid of it). Don't even think about saying "Computers are not for me." I don't care if you don't have a computer, don't want one and think the whole computer thing is a passing fad. To turn your back on the treasure that is the Internet is to starve your precious dreams to death.

To dump that old conventional wisdom, do some Internet research: Interview anyone who works (or plays) in the field you want to explore by heading over to Google and typing in anything that interests you – from beekeeping to xylophones. You'll be amazed and delighted!

(Can't afford a computer? Find an inexpensive Internet café, or go to your public library where they'll help you navigate this new technology. Or search your newspaper for refurbished computers. Don't know what to buy or how to use it? Get on the phone with a teenage relative anywhere in the world. They'll usually help you without a thought. No relatives? Contact your local high school principal and ask for help from a student.) OK, no more excuses. Now get connected.

Tip 18: Empty your thinking of the "Either-Or" fallacy

A client recently said to me, "I have no idea what career I want. I just know I don't want a life stocking shelves with canned soup."

Well, *that's* a start. But don't assume it's your Dream Job vs. the Pits of Hell. Do you have any idea how many people would never even *think* of such an alternative? This kind of thinking blinds you to so many other options.

Like, how about your dream job vs. a *pleasant* job, surrounded by nice co-workers, that leaves you the time and brings you the money to do your most beloved activity on your own? Or how about having 3 or 4 *different* ways of bringing in money, where *one* of them involves doing what you love best? Or, if your dream is to live in another country, how about getting a temporary job of *any* kind – in that country?

Just take the most unbearable jobs *off* all your option lists. Who said those were your choices? The most radical notions are the most frightening. Too many people scare themselves with choices that don't make any sense, like "I'd have to quit my job and let my family starve if I became a scuba diver."

In fact, if you *really* became a scuba diver, you'd either find a way to earn money at it, or you'd do it part of the time and earn money the rest of the time. If you avoid 'Either-Or" thinking, you'll be much more willing to go after your dreams.

Tip 19: Never wait until you have "more time"

Pardon me for sounding negative but something bad could happen and your dream could be snatched away at the eleventh hour. One client of mine worked almost every waking minute and saw her dream of being an artist waiting 8 years in the distance, when she'd be retiring. As far as I'm concerned, waiting that long for something you want is just tempting fate.

Since she wasn't in a position to retire early, I persuaded her to start on her dream at once, taking one evening class a week. To do it, she arranged to leave work one hour early, one day a week – something she had once thought impossible because her work load was so heavy. But now she finds herself working more efficiently so she can get to her art class.

"Not only am I happier than I've been in years," she wrote me, "but when the time comes to retire, I'll already be a working artist, not just a beginner."

Take my advice: don't wait for anything. Start right now.

Tip 20: Don't compare yourself to anyone

You can't write like James Joyce? Well, he couldn't write like Shakespeare! And neither of them could write like you can. Whenever you do what you love, you become an original (see Tip 14). When you listen to the talent that's planted in you courtesy of Nature, you're always breaking new ground and comparisons are irrelevant.

I've heard established writers say of a novice's work, "I wish I'd written that." They know very well that art is never complete and new beauty is always appearing. If you're an artist, it's your obligation to add to it in your own unique way. And you *are* an artist, no matter what you do, because your art is what you create while you're on this planet, and that means your life is your work of art.

Tip 21: Don't automatically believe the experts

It never hurts to get advice from people in the field, but don't buy their answers wholesale. Experts make mistakes too, big ones, because they often ignore good sense.

When I was in college the experts insisted that the continents had never been attached, they just looked like they had. (They were wrong.) They also said animals didn't have feelings, and doing sit-ups was good for your back. (Wrong again – twice.) I hear the experts have recently reversed themselves on their pronouncements about the virtues of using a very hard toothbrush.

Listen to them – the wise person learns from everyone – but remember they're only human. Be wary of going against your own judgment; the final word is never in, and you just might know more than they do.

Tip 22: Don't save the fun for later

Even if it's only for 5 minutes a day, always do what you *love to do* right in the middle of all the hard work you *have to do*. Don't do it first (you'll never want to do your work at all!) and don't do it last (hard work has a way of never ending, and you could drop from exhaustion before your dream gets its turn).

Instead, as soon as you start feeling tired, take a delicious 5-minute visit into anything you love. Put down your paid work and read from your favorite book, write a line or two for a song, or work on the design for your garden. It will refresh your mind and help you get through the hard work much more efficiently. It will also remind you why you're working so hard in the first place!

Tip 23: Forget the 'lonely artist' stance

Don't wait until you have that cabin in the woods to produce your masterpiece.

Someone once said to me, "For such a long time I wanted to write novels, and I think about stories all the time, but I get stuck when I sit down to actually write. I can never figure out how to start, or I decide my idea is lousy and I lose confidence. I thought setting aside some time to write and going off by myself would have helped, but it hasn't. Why don't I follow through?"

People say this about every kind of dream – not just writing – because doing something creative or new is like walking into unknown territory. It's scary. And it's hard to be inspired when you're scared and alone. The fear in you will try to stop you with anything it can find (for example, whispering in your ear that your idea is worthless).

The solution is to *end your isolation.* If you're serious about turning out some work, you need to have someone waiting to see it. You need to know you have work that is due by a certain time. You need accountability. Accountability is what makes you pay your taxes and keep your dentist appointments.

So, take a class, join a group, get a coach or a writing buddy, and meet on a regular basis to show your work. You'll be taking steps toward your dream every week. And you'll do it without waiting for anything.

Tip 24: Know when you're being manipulated

A manipulator can throw you and your dream way off track, so it's important to be able to spot one right away. If someone is trying to get you to do something you don't want to do – something you sense is not right for you – watch them carefully. Don't argue, just start taking mental notes. Instead of responding to a comment that makes you feel uncomfortable, pay attention.

You might hear very convincing arguments, but if you're arguing back, you've already given too much power to a manipulator. Back away from being in debate mode and look behind the words to the debater.

Why is he promoting something you don't want to do? Would you ask another person to do the same thing? If not, you're being manipulated. You don't need to prove you're right. Just say, "I'm not comfortable doing that. Thanks anyway." And let them say anything they like.

They'll probably ask "Why?" so they can get you back into debate mode, but don't be tempted to explain. Just smile and nod slightly like you're missing a few I.Q. points or you've just lost the power of speech. Don't be drawn onto their turf no matter how odd you think your behavior looks. If they persist in trying to influence you, look at your watch and say, "Well, I have to go now," and walk away.

Manipulators have their own reasons for wanting to interrupt your dreams. But your dreams are more important than any of them.

Tip 25: Ignore your feelings of being mediocre

"What if I become an architect and discover I'm only average?" I've heard versions of that sentence more times than I can count. The short answer is, if you love architecture you *can't* be mediocre. It's impossible.

However, if you're working to show the world you're as good as the famous architects (or painters, designers, athletes, writers) you're in big trouble, because unless you work for the love of it, you'll never be able to tap the one-of-a-kind talent that's in you.

Anyway, you never have any control over how the world sees you. Even the "great" ones fall in and out of favor with every new generation. Turn your ranking in the Hall of Fame over to fate and think only about how you want to spend your life on this earth.

How will you feel when you're designing a hillside retreat (if you're an architect)? If that's not your dream, how will you feel when you're singing, sewing, building, traveling, debating, skiing, or putting a shine on your sailboat? Will you feel like a mediocre person? Will you feel like a superior person? When you're doing what you really love, those words lose their meaning. You won't even remember them.

Tip 26: Respect even your wildest dream

Even if your dream looks completely out of reach, hold on to it with respect and interest. You and everyone around you might think it's impossible but *you don't know what's possible.* One thing is certain: the elements that matter most to you are *always* attainable!

Realistic or not, your dream wouldn't exist unless you had a very good reason for letting it live in your heart. Dreams are messages sent from talent, they're longings for something that you need. So never take them lightly. They deserve your keenest attention.

One day they'll make perfect sense to you.

Tip 27: Be a verb, not a noun

Never think of yourself as a thing, or focus on how good or bad you look. Change from a named object into a series of actions. Labels are for things that can't move, things that are owned by the beholder, the person who is looking at them.

You are capable of learning, building, creating, teaching, interpreting, repairing, planting, questioning, praising, defending – and a thousand other actions.

You belong to yourself. You're not a beautiful thing or a bad thing, not a profession or a title, not even a hero -- or a parent! You should quit trying to look like your label just as you should quit trying to act your age. Maintaining an image is like pinning yourself to a board in a butterfly collection.

Instead of posing for an imaginary camera or performing for an invisible audience, take your life back *by getting into action*. *Move* after what you want. *Do* what you care about. *Learn* about what interests you. *Fight* for what matters to you.

Even seeing – really seeing – is a powerful action. And if people persist in labeling you, ignore them and don't even *consider* freezing into conformity. You have *exciting* work to do.

Tip 28: Exploit any benefits of hard luck right away

Got ditched by someone? Laid up? Laid off? I'm not saying you should be cheerful about bad events, but you should start exploiting the benefits that came along with the disaster, specifically those benefits that might contribute to finding your dreams. Are you finally in the mood to write poetry? Do you find yourself with more time than you've had for years?

Use this opportunity to go after a dream instead of wasting your time bemoaning your bad luck. Bad luck never lasts. Soon enough you'll have another job or another love and this unusual open space in your life will be gone. So make it count. Come out of this period with new ideas, acquaintances, experiences that you can use when things get back to 'normal'.

Tip 29: Don't fake being "above" insults and outrages

Fight back or the misdeed will stay inside you. Too many people say they just don't want to bother confronting people who have done something wrong; that they don't want to "stoop to their level." But allowing people to get away with bad behavior is irresponsible on your part: they'll just do the same thing to the next person.

One way of making your world better is to throw them off balance so they think twice before doing it again. How? Just quietly call them on their behavior. Without anger, without a smile, say something like, "That wasn't very nice," and look at them calmly. Seems mild, doesn't it? But it always shocks unkind people to have their behavior brought out into the open. No matter how they respond, they know they've lost the battle and usually won't try it again.

Tip 30: If you're curious about something, go looking for answers

If you've ever asked yourself, "How do they find such great locations for movies?" "Can anyone become a public speaker?" or "What's all this talk about building straw bale houses?" go looking for information now.

Don't live with ignorance and don't worry about being scattered. Trust your curiosity. It has its own reasons. Anyway, knowledge is like money: you can always find a use for it someday. So get accustomed to taking a little time to follow through on anything that interests you.

It's easier than you think. You can ask your friends via email or phone, or do a search on the Internet. You can look in an encyclopedia or the *Reader's Guide to Periodical Literature* at your local library, but take a few minutes to get those fleeting questions answered.

It's a good habit to develop for many reasons, one being self-esteem: if you want to know something, you deserve to know it.

You might want to write what you learn in a "day book." That way new thoughts and discoveries can be found if you need them. You'll be surprised how valuable fulfilled curiosity can be.

Tip 31: Don't stay too long in a toxic environment

Don't stay in a toxic scene so long you become too ill to leave. A job you hate and dread will weaken you day by day. Don't assume you can leave "some day." Start preparing for your move today and stay on that project every day. Even the preparation will make the job less toxic. It will also remind you that you have a future and that you're taking steps to make it a good one.

Tip 32: Decide that you intend to find out what your dream is

Searching for your dream requires a decision. Sounds simple, but many people overlook it and stay in a general wistful wishing mode. Roll up your sleeves and declare to yourself that this is your project.

As soon as you find what your dream is you can get to work on it, but you can't make a move until then. So make the decision: you're not just going to passively wish that you knew what you really wanted. You're going to go looking.

Tip 33: Don't weigh your dreams down with non-essentials

One reason dreams are hard to uncover is that you may have strapped all kinds of requirements to them – requirements that aren't at all necessary. I know someone who wants her own philanthropy, but she's decided that she needs to be a multi-millionaire to do it. Here are the facts (I know because I have a philanthropy of my own): 1) You can start a philanthropy with very little money, and 2) Philanthropies that require millions look for outside funding, anyway.

Trying to get rich can eat up a lot of time and is by no means guaranteed. It would be smarter to create her philanthropy on a very small scale first, and try to get rich second – or not at all.

Like the retired woman I heard about, living in a poor section of town, who started using as much of her social security check as she could to cook up hearty soups. Then she took them downstairs to a small table where she sat and handed out bowls of soup every day.

Her daughter, who was a relatively successful minor executive in some company downtown, started helping her. Eventually she left her job and started working full-time with her mother. They opened up a storefront so people could come indoors in the winter, play checkers, read the papers, even get instructions in reading or filling out forms.

Tip 34: Do a search for the essentials of your dream

What would really satisfy you? No one knows the answer to that but you, and the only way for you to find out is to ask yourself: what is the heart of my dream, the most important part? That's the key to everything. Once you know the essentials, you won't make any mistakes or commit to the wrong path.

However, you must be prepared to find anything, even if you can't defend it with logic or good sense. Love is never rational and isn't supposed to be. But never forget that what you love is what you are gifted at, and only your feelings can guide you to your gifts. Once you've found your dream, you can rally your powers of reason to defend it.

Tip 35: Listen for your talent

You're not free to decide where you'll be talented. That information already exists, and it's your job to discover it. The evidence is all around you. Listen with respect and don't strong-arm the data.

Start noting all the things you enjoy most – the things you love to look at or do, the things that are fun or appealing - and keep a list. Then invite your friends (and their friends) over to your place one evening and tell everyone what's on it. Someone there might know exactly what talents your list reveals and how you might be able to use them.

Tip 36: Stand up for your dream

Decide to be the champion for your dream, even before you've found it. Take a position. Pledge to protect it with everything you've got. Promise to respect everyone's dreams, especially your own, on principle.

Tip 37: Don't assume the obvious

If you loved history until you left that one great class, maybe your gift isn't history at all; maybe it's learning from great teachers. If you've always loved dogs, don't assume you have to be a veterinarian, and if you love to cook, don't assume you have to be a chef or own a restaurant.

We make the jump too fast from what we love to the most obvious career it points to. Slow down. Keep your eye on what you love most about your dream, not what you think a career counselor might suggest you do with it.

Tip 38: Admit you don't have the answers and try things out

Some assumptions look so logical we never bother to confirm them, or ask ourselves how reliable the source was. And most of the time we don't even remember where we got our information. Mistaken assumptions kill any further inquiry and waste a lot of time. The wisest thing to do is admit you don't know the answers. Then you can go after the information you need with an open mind. Look at this letter I got recently:

"I always assumed that being a filmmaker would require huge amounts of money and endless schooling, so I never gave it a try. And I figured wannabe filmmakers were so numerous, so why would I be the special one? I never bothered to check out the reality. Instead, I became a film historian and taught in a community college for years.

Finally I took a filmmaking course, found (of course) that I had a real flair for movie making, and am now doing my dream, making documentaries about the neighborhoods in my town. This is my real dream and guess what? It's earning money! I've sold two pieces to my local public TV station and one to a university film department, and I've been approached by an association to make a film of their neighborhood."

Tip 39: Expect some of your gifts to be receptive, not active

You might find your talent lies in being able to see and enjoy things on a more intense level than most people. You can always use that talent to be a reviewer or a consultant, but you don't have to turn every gift into a career. Sometimes the greatest joy in life is simply feeling the impact of something you have the special senses to appreciate.

"I've always followed my interests and jumped into them with enthusiasm. A few years ago I acknowledged how much I love houses and homes and concluded I should be in real estate. When that didn't seem like much fun I thought, perhaps I should be a builder. Or design homes, like an architect.

Looking into all those fields made me realize I didn't want to sell houses, or build or design them either. I just loved looking at them, seeing them as if they were characters, beautiful but with personalities and stories like a person. So, to make myself happy I take photos or make sketches and mount them in a scrapbook, just for myself, so I'll remember how lovely the houses were.

Every now and then I take it out and look through it and it makes me feel wonderful. Last weekend I showed the pictures to a 7-year old niece and made up a story of the house and the family that lived in it and we both had a great time!"

Tip 40: Follow every lead: You have no idea what will show itself

Don't limit your search to the predictable. When something attracts you for no apparent reason, be a good detective: pay attention and make no attempt to explain or justify it prematurely. Respect the process of learning something new.

Even if this new interest is a diversionary tactic by your subconscious to pull you off track, it still has valuable elements in it. Make note of it, put it away and get back to work on your main project. But don't disregard a rush of interest that seems irrelevant. You may well be discovering something new about yourself, and the pieces will make sense in good time.

Tip 41: Park your judgmental self outside

The judge inside you criticizes just about anything you do. Everyone knows about that. But did you ever wonder what he's doing there? You put him there yourself early in life to defend yourself from critics, oddly enough.

Your internal judge is the one who knocks your ideas down before someone else gets the chance. You gave him the exact words and attitude you expected to be used against you, and that gave you a feeling of being in control, untrickable.

Unfortunately, this defense turns out to be an enemy that kills more dreams than any outside critic can. Your internal judge has so many restraining orders on your dreams they can't get near enough to grab your attention. If you're hearing pompous or self-righteous voices inside you that sound suspiciously like some critic or belittler in your past, don't defend yourself. See if you can trick them into stepping outside your head for a while - then lock the door. A little phrase like this might work: "I know this idea of mine isn't going to lead anywhere, but I'm going to check it out just for the fun of it." That will appease the critics long enough for you to get back to work.

Tip 42: Don't ask for advice from people who don't know anything

Everybody's an expert at the dinner table, but it's very unlikely they have real experience in the area you want to pursue. Even if they have some background, they might not understand anything new or original you want to do.

You can't get the help you need from people who know even less than you do. There is no other way to find your gifts except by listening to your feelings and following up with a search for some real information.

"I abandoned my dream of being a journalist without even giving it a try, just because everyone said you can't make a living that way. I didn't even check out the details very much, just gave the dream up.

I also liked law school (because I was influenced by a TV series, like a lot of other people) and was told that was the dream to listen to. Unfortunately, I did. It took 14 years to make the switch to journalism, years that were unhappy ones. If I had it to do it over, I'd listen to my own heart and ignore everyone else."

Tip 43: If something is truly impossible, do it a different way

I constantly meet innovators who did something so new that everyone wondered why it hadn't been thought of before. When I ask them how they became so original they all say nearly the same thing: "I saw I couldn't have what I wanted if I did things the usual way. So I thought up a different way to do them." Necessity is the mother of invention. If something can't be done one way, invent another.

"I love to learn new things and I always knew I wanted to teach people in a way so they'd love learning too, but I just couldn't take the courses in the education department. They seemed like the only boring classes in the whole college curriculum! I studied art and history and geology and math, everything excited me. But I never got a teaching credential.

I became a teacher's assistant and found I wouldn't have liked being a real teacher after all. Too regimented for me. So I became a motivational speaker! I just did it on the side at first, while I worked in an office. I gave free speeches on how great it is to be alive as long as you never stop learning.

I was invited to give talks at a local community center for senior citizens. I was so enthusiastic and had such good results that people helped me put together my first tour of community centers and senior centers all over the state and now I train people from all over the country to do what I do."

Tip 44: Be prepared to upset somebody

At a recent TV appearance, a young man working with the producer stepped forward and told me, "You'll like my story. I was in med school and hated it. So I dropped out, picked up a band and started cutting records and traveling around the country! We're actually supporting ourselves and doing rather well. And I'm very happy."

I was delighted but couldn't resist asking, "How's your Dad feeling?" He laughed. "My parents went ballistic, and at first I was surprised. I thought my life was supposed to be about me being happy, not fulfilling their expectations. But I stuck to my guns and kept reminding them how unhappy I was in med school.

They came around in time, and were great about it, but they admit they're still amazed that I'm doing so well. I realize they were just afraid I was going to be broke and miserable. Now I think they're going to use all that med school money on themselves! How's that for win-win?" he smiled.

Tip 45: Don't be a snob toward what you love

If you love acting or making jewelry or working outdoors in a state park, but everyone in your family is a Federal judge or dedicated academic, a cop or a financier, you might have to fight them to get the respect you deserve, but don't fight yourself.

If you're from an artist's or social worker's family and all you want is to buy and sell businesses and make gobs of money, you have to make sure you, too, are not looking down on your dream. If you insist on being a snob, you won't be able to hear your dream when it calls to you, because you've been taught not to respect it.

Consider your dream to be your long-lost child who has finally found you. Welcome it and give it a home. One day you'll understand how remarkable it really is. Maybe the others will too. But that's not really what's important.

Tip 46: Don't defend your dream to other snobs

If you're surrounded by snobs – or you have to meet them at birthdays and holidays – it will be hard not to be affected by their opinions. You may understand that they simply lack the ability (or the willingness) to understand why you're following a dream so "beneath your abilities" or so "impractical." But their attitude gets under your skin anyway and puts you in the unenviable position of having a discussion that will go nowhere.

It's time for a trick, and here's my favorite: Call your dream a hobby. Tell them it helps you focus or it relaxes you. Then engage them in a truly passionate discussion of trivia about your "hobby" and watch them try to get away. The result: you don't have to waste your time defending yourself to people who just don't get it. They don't care about your dumb hobbies, so there's nothing to discuss.

Tip 47: Don't waste precious time trying to please a chronically discontented person

People who tell you something's wrong, but will never let you try to fix it, are doing a private dance that they need to do. It has nothing to do with you, and that's not what you were put here for. You have work to do and if you wait for them to be happy, it will never get done.

If you have a chronically discontented person in your life, throw them a curve ball they don't expect. Instead of shouldering their problem, give them the respect (and give yourself the distance) of saying with complete concern: "Wow, that's terrible! What are you going to do?" If they say, "I don't know," just answer, "You're so smart. You'll think of something."

Give sympathy, not advice. That might be all they want. If not, they'll try to pull you back into the dance, so be sure to stay out of reach. Don't be egotistical enough to assume you can fix their problem.

Tip 48: Don't count your blessings. Look for what's missing

Something isn't there. Something that would make your life more satisfying is missing. Don't silence your discontent by counting your blessings! There's something you need and it's calling to you. One client told me she was dissatisfied, even though she had a beautiful home, a wonderful husband and a prestigious job.

"What's missing?" I asked.

"I don't know! I have everything I ever wanted," she said hopelessly.

"If this was all you were ever going to get until the end of your life, where would the hole in your life be?"

She almost started to cry. "I want to live closer to my family, my parents and my brothers and sisters. We had such a great time together."

"Is it out of the question to live closer to them?" I asked.

"I don't know," she said, a little surprised. "My husband's work can be done from anywhere because he travels all the time. And he loves my family, too. But I don't know if I can keep my career."

"How important is your career to you?"

She looked as if she was revealing a shameful secret when she said, "It's not important at all. It looks good and it makes money but it doesn't mean a thing to me."

She and her husband now live near her family in New England and she's gotten another job, a reasonably good one that she likes as much as the one she left. It makes less money, but it also uses up less of her time, leaving her more time for her family. She also finds she doesn't spend as much as she used to when she was discontented and lonely.

Tip 49: Don't announce your new dream to the whole world

Often when we discover our dreams we're so excited that we run to everyone and tell them, assuming they'll be equally in love with our idea. But even supportive friends can't always understand what you're talking about, and when a dream is new, it's often hard to defend. Just a look of incomprehension in their eyes might take the wind out of your sails.

New dreams are like infants. They deserve to do a little growing before they're evaluated. So even before you discover what your dream is, make a quiet declaration that you'll keep it to yourself until it's stronger. (Be especially careful not to tell people who might belittle it.)

Tip 50: Be prepared to search your childhood for clues

Gifts are genetic, which means they left plenty of clues in your childhood. If you think you can't remember your childhood, start asking relatives what you liked to do as a little kid (ask soon while they're still around). Don't be shy about calling distant relatives. Ask if they can remember anything about you as a kid, even hearsay.

Here's a neat trick: pretend you're any age under 12 – say, 4 years old. Now, as that child, look around you. Where are you (playground/ beach/ grandparents' house)? In that setting, what gives you the greatest pleasure? Imagine you're actually doing the activities you loved and try to figure out exactly what you loved about them. Those are the best clues in the world for discovering your gifts.

Tip 51: Stop fearing negativity

If you take negativity the right way, it can be quite amusing. Besides, negativity, like any problem, doesn't go away by just pretending it's not there. In fact, you give it much more power than it deserves by fearing it.

Instead, create a "Life is Hell" notebook, or throw a "Life is Hell" party and be as negative as you like. Ask for applause from friends if you do an especially good job of explaining why everything is terrible. Let them join in, too.

Tip 52: Promise yourself you'll follow what you love – no matter what it may be

Without that promise, your dreams won't come out of hiding. Why should they? They've probably done it before and been driven underground by your fear or self-doubt. Your dreams are important. They're not just rewards for having worked hard, they're the core of who you are and must be respected.

Remember, you don't have to earn a living from your dreams, or walk out on your present life to live them. But you must follow them and bring them into your life. So, be on the lookout for any sign of what you love to do, and promise never to turn your back on a dream when it appears.

Tip 53: Need motivation? Where will you be in 5 years?

It's hard to get out of a rut and into a high-energy activity. No one can blame you for putting it off. But time is not endless. If you need something to propel you into action, take a look at the calendar. Where will you be 5 years from now?

And how will you feel if the answer is, "Exactly where I am right now"?

"I found myself aching to spend time building furniture, a dream of mine since college. I've always had these wonderful ideas, but putting it off became a habit. I'd learn how to make furniture after the children were grown, when the holidays were over, after someone's graduation.

But when I turned 50 I woke up and became aware of my mortality. I just signed up for a class from a master furniture designer. It begins in 2 months. I haven't been this excited in years and I don't know why I didn't start before. 50 seems kind of old to me, but I realized I don't want to turn 55 without making beautiful chairs and tables with my own hands. I don't know how much time I have, but I want to make the most of whatever it will be."

He's wrong about 50 being late in life for new projects, but he'll realize that, once he's doing what he loves. My mother started getting into the Internet when she was almost 90!

Tip 54: Take another look at dreams you once vetoed

Something you once loved may have gotten rejected for the wrong reasons. If you loved those dreams once, there must be a good reason. Look at them again.

"I always loved to fix things: clocks, plumbing, small appliances, and I always knew it. As a little kid I said I was going to be an electrician when I grew up. But then I went to college, and nothing seemed more inappropriate than fixing things for a living. Who becomes a handyman with a college degree? It's like being a loser.

So I made it a hobby, and enjoyed myself helping neighbors with their lawnmowers, until I realized that people were bringing their cars to me, and their TV sets, and offering to pay good money for me to fix them. I have a special "ear" apparently. I know how to listen to little machines and hear the problem. I'm making so much money at handyman repairs now, I can realistically think about leaving a corporate job I detest to open my own business."

Tip 55: Pay attention to fun: It's scientific data

Fun isn't silly or frivolous; it's solid data that will lead you to your gifts. Analyze what kinds of projects you do for fun and you'll know which skills you should develop (because those are the skills you'll always enjoy and be good at). What you discover will leave you with no doubt about where you'll be special, more insightful, more innovative, and more sure of yourself.

"I didn't take what I loved very seriously because I thought it was just silly stuff I did for fun."

When something is fun for you it means you have special abilities in that area, or you wouldn't enjoy it so much. You make a huge mistake if you ignore things because they're "only" done for fun. Take a look at what's fun for you and you'll find where your gifts lie. They're always nearby.

Tip 56: Check to see if you withheld doing what you loved on purpose

Did you turn away from what you would have loved in order to get even with someone who was unkind, or to keep control of your life from someone who didn't understand boundaries? Take a look. If you're someone who always seems to be working under your potential, that might be the reason. If you become conscious of having held yourself back deliberately to punish someone who hurt you long ago, you might get your life handed back to you.

"I never knew why I continually sabotaged myself until I remembered what was behind it one really important time, and it changed everything. My family never supported what I did. They either didn't care or made fun of me. I paid my own way through college and worked my way up in my field in science, which was hard for a woman at the time.

But I had some friends in my department who begged me to apply for a special award they were convinced I deserved and could get, and this award would have assured my place in my field. Somehow my family got wind of it and all of a sudden I was a big hero. They made a fuss, told all their friends, called me on the phone to say how proud they were of me.

And then I missed the deadline. It was really stupid, I never knew how that happened. But when you asked that question, I remembered how I felt when I saw them finally being happy about what I did. Something in me went stone cold. All I could think of was that they would take credit for my award, and they didn't deserve it. And I refused to apply. I didn't forget. I just couldn't do it."

Tip 57: Create tricks to find time

Make appointments you might actually keep (but where no one is depending on you) and at the last minute, cancel them. (Feels like found time! Works great with big chunks of time – like 5 days!) Resolve to clean your closets and then at the last minute, don't do it. (They'll only get messed up again, and you know it.)

Use the new time to do something special, something connected with your dream, like set up a table with all the materials you need to make a model village, or create a corner where you can read the books you love most, or go on the Internet and find a walking map of somewhere you've been longing to go (and maybe order some walking shoes while you're at it.)

But what if there are things that have to be done or your home will stop functioning? Those are time-consuming but someone has to do them. Fair enough. Hire someone. If you have no time to follow your dream, you should make an important promise to yourself: that you will never waste time doing something that someone else can do. Where will you get the money to pay them? Find it.

Sell something. Stop buying something. Find a non-time-consuming way to make a little extra cash.

Too many people think it's self-indulgent to hire someone to help with chores. That means you plan to devote your life to housekeeping, not your gifts. Get your priorities lined up better. Your gifts need your attention (and the person you hire needs the money).

Tip 58: Turn your assumptions into questions

If you've done a lot of things that weren't satisfying, you might be locked into a certain kind of thinking – like, "I have to have a job with *some* company although I've always hated the corporate world," or "I have to work in the travel field because I love travel, but every job I've taken in that field made me unhappy."

You need to launch a search and destroy mission for mistaken assumptions that stand between you and what you'd love to do. Turn every assumption into a question: "Why does a job have to be with a company?", or "Why does a job have to be indoors?", or "Why don't I earn my money in a number of small ways and forget having a job at all?", or "Why do I have to have a job in the travel industry? Why don't I get (or create) a job that gives me enough time and money to travel on my own?"

A client of mine (who worked in finance) remembered that in school his best moments were his art classes, and said to me, "My dream is to work in the art field." But after looking at every possible way he could do that he said, "No, none of those interest me. I don't want to represent artists, or advise them, or manage their money. I don't even want to paint!"

Further questioning showed that what he loved most was listening to artists talk about art. He loved hanging out and talking with them because their thinking was so fresh and stimulating to him. A little more searching turned up an unexpected gem: he loved *all* learning. He loved it like a natural athlete loves physical movement. Art was only one area that could give him the kind of fresh, new learning he loved. Now he audits courses at a local university whenever he can, choosing his courses by how interesting the professor is.

So, make sure to flip over every assumption you've made about doing what you love (or why you're not doing it) and see what it turns up: you might be a lot closer than you realize.

Tip 59: Identify the right form for your dream

In writing, it is said, the material finds its own form. You can't cram a novel into a short story, or turn a play into a magazine article. The same is true of a dream. Until the form shows itself to you, it's very hard to proceed – and heaven help you if you pick the wrong form.

One of my clients (whom I shall call Alice) loved fabric and clothing design, so she assumed she needed a store of her own. She got one, but found that she had to work 70 hours a week and almost never got to do the part she really loved the most: finding unusual fabrics and designing the clothes that were exactly right for that fabric.

"Having a store is so expensive. Rent and advertising and employees cost so much money, that I have to generate a lot of income and have no time to do what I love," she said

A retail store was not the right form for Alice's dream. Together we searched for a better one. Alice really wanted to be a dress designer. But this created a new problem. Using the typical business model for fashion designers she would need to risk a lot of money.

The solution was to invent a new form: Alice has assembled a mailing list of all her clients and when she has a new line ready to sell, she invites them to her home to see the fabrics and try on samples. When they find what they want, they pay for their orders and leave. In a week or two, their new clothes arrive in the mail.

So, before you go renting a store (or enrolling in Med school or even accepting a job at NASA!), make sure that this form will actually fulfill your dream. How? Try this surefire technique I use with my clients: first, create your dream in any form you choose and imagine you are actually there. If it's a store, open the doors, check the inventory and the cash register, talk to a customer, call a supplier.

Now, as you go through every step, carefully note how you feel. On a scale of 1 to 10, see how happy each element makes you. Take anything that doesn't make you happy – anything that's a 6 or below on that scale – and change it to something you like better. Then go through the fantasy again and repeat the process until everything feels good.

It takes a little time but if you do it, you really can design a form that will work perfectly for you. You still have to make it happen, of course, but now you'll have a good blueprint for how to proceed (and, just as important, how *not* to).

Tip 60: Check to see if an old battle is blocking your vision

For example, was there someone you were afraid to compete with? You might be surprised to find you know perfectly well what you'd love to do, but have discounted it because long ago you feared competing with a sibling or a parent.

Ask yourself this question: "If I had no early emotional conflicts at all, what would I have wanted?" Your dream might appear as plain as day, and you might even think, "I knew that! Why didn't I remember that?" The answer: an old habit of thinking persisted after it was no longer relevant. Turning the light on it makes your dream visible again.

If you still find yourself conflicted, in spite of your most rational explanations to yourself about how it's over and doesn't matter anymore, that means you have to bring that history front and center. Now answer these questions:

– How old were you when you felt that way?

– What happened between you and this person since that time?

– How hard was it for the child you were to turn his or her back on that dream?

It's time to give some sympathy and compassion to the child who authored that early decision never to compete: tell them they can relax now, and that you'll take care of everything from now on. (Don't be afraid to let out any emotions that come up. They'll make it easier to break free of your past.)

Tip 61: Look for self-protective behavior getting in your way

For example, did you hide your abilities so people would take care of you? I call that 'learned helplessness'. You don't see it too often, so it gets overlooked. But with great talent sometimes comes great fear, and you may be hiding all kinds of competence to maintain a habit of being taken care of. If you're actually scared, you'd better find out where the danger is and do something about it.

It's also possible that you're no longer scared at all; you're just in the habit of pulling caretakers into your life. Being taken care of requires you to be passive, and that's a bad state of mind when going after a dream. Being carried means accommodating your caretaker, and it never gives you the same freedom that walking on your own does. Start practicing by picking yourself up when you fall and see if you can develop a taste for it.

Tip 62: Search for a painful drama in the back of your thinking

For example, was there someone you felt terribly sorry for when you were young? If you know the answer without thinking too much, you might want to look in that area to find out why you think you shouldn't go after your dreams.

You might be one of those people who started thinking very early on that it was selfish to ask for more when you were already so lucky. That's a kind of children's magic: anything you get comes off someone else's plate. You may even get some satisfaction in thinking you're doing some good by not giving yourself real happiness. But grownups know that sacrificing your dreams doesn't make any difference to someone else who can't have theirs.

Sally always thought that realizing her dream of traveling through Asia would hurt her sister, who married early and never had the chance to travel. After a long period of feeling guilty about her dream, she had a conversation with her sister before giving it up altogether. It turned out that the sister never wanted what Sally wanted, and was very happy with her own life. Now Sally sends postcards and artifacts from all over, which are a huge hit with her sister's kids.

Tip 63: Check to see if you're under pressure to live up to others' expectations

You can't find out what you love when your mind is crowded with noisy people telling you what to do. Maybe someone wants (or wanted) you to be something for their sake (see Tip 56). Or maybe you only think they do. In either case, something or someone is interrupting your natural impulse to activate your inborn talents.

Someone important to you, now or in your past, wasn't aware of those talents, or didn't value them. But that doesn't let you off the hook. You owe your very best to the world, to the rest of us, and you can only do your very best by doing what's most enjoyable, satisfying and fun for you.

Tip 64: Argue in favor of conformity, tradition and belonging

Build a case to prove that conformity and tradition are the foundation of all that is stable and solid – that belonging to the people you were raised among has a value that mavericks will never appreciate. Make a good case. If you find yourself resisting, make the case even better. (If you do this easily, move to the next page.)

Why should you do this? Well, if you've been raised in a conventional family you might think you have to reject them in order to go after your dreams. That would be a shame, because you need some of the nourishment that comes with their point of view. Don't worry: it isn't an all-or-nothing decision. You'll last longer as an original if you take in the solidity of your background along with the exploration of the life you're building.

If you avoid your people because they so often want a debate about your lifestyle versus theirs, don't give it to them. Just tell them they're wonderful as they are and you love them. That will confuse them so much they'll have to give up their fight. And anyway, it's true.

Tip 65: Argue in favor of innovation, the bohemian life and freedom

You don't have to bother with this one unless you're someone who really dislikes bohemians (because they seem irresponsible, or because you once were like them and have become more conventional as you got older). But if you're feeling a bit defensive about being conventional, make a case for being a hippy.

Don't worry, you won't have to sleep in the streets or live in an attic. What you might do, however – while keeping those parts of your nice life that matter to you – is take a history class, or learn a language you don't need, or take up singing, and understand that you don't have to live either the conventional life or the bohemian life, because you're going to live *your* life.

Tip 66: Don't assume that because you can't do what you love right now, you can't do it ever

"I had debts to pay off, so I couldn't just jump into what I wanted. I decided to give up and do something more practical. That wasn't such a bad idea, but for some reason I decided it was forever. I should have continued to do what I loved a little every day until the time came that those debts were paid off and I could do it full time!"

There's no time limit on your special gifts. They will always be there as long as you keep them alive in your thinking, ready to be picked up when you're ready. Can't go trekking in Nepal this summer? Keep a photo of Katmandu on your desk to remind you of where you'll be when next summer rolls around.

Tip 67: Try before you buy

"I'd love to be a teacher, but I'm not sure if I'm ready to make such a big commitment." There's no way to know if something you love will be your life's calling until you try it out.

Rather than raising the stakes so high in your mind, it makes more sense to get some experience without those big expectations, and then see how you feel about it. It might be everything you need, or a wonderful part of the life you want. Or it might lead you in a totally new, fascinating direction. But you shouldn't be thinking in the long term until you get your feet wet. Rent first: you can always buy later.

If you want your talent to become a career, you should expect to try out more than one career just to see how it feels. Every real experience you have will tell you more about what you love and what you don't, what excites you and what bores you. And it's hard to get this information by just thinking about it. You have to get out there to see what it's really like.

Tip 68: Appreciate being a grownup

Forget Peter Pan. He was created (by a grownup, incidentally) during a time when adults had a very odd notion of childhood. The idea that it's horrible to be a grownup comes from the mistaken notion that children are radiantly happy because they don't have to pay taxes, and that there's something wrong with having a driver's license and freedom of choice.

Being a grownup is great. Enjoy it!

Tip 69: Learn to admire reality

A real apple tastes better than a magic one. Don't blind yourself to the delights of the real world by gazing only at an ideal world. There's nothing wrong with having an exalted dream as long as you respect the richness and complexity of what you have now. Admire the magic of reality.

Tip 70: Find a job title to match your favorite skills

Remember, we're not talking about a dream job, just a job that pays the bills and doesn't drive you crazy. If you search for that kind of job, you open an interesting new arena: jobs that can be fun.

Skills aren't the same as dreams, but if you're allowed to use the skills you enjoy most, you can get a very pleasant "day job" while building your dream. I had a session with someone who called himself a "glorified secretary." He was in charge of making appointments, booking plane flights, ordering office supplies, etc. in a small section of a large corporation.

"Drives me crazy," he said. "Such a waste of my time, and no appreciation." He was looking for a dream career that used his people skills. "I love to show people how to make things work, how to get out of their own way, etc. I want to teach, but not in a school, and not for a small paycheck." In the meantime, he needed a job that wasn't hard on him. After fishing around a little bit, we found that one of the skills he enjoys using is keeping his home incredibly organized and clean.

"If you have people skills, you like to teach and you enjoy keeping things organized and running well, you're an office manager," I said. "And if you're as good as you sound, a smart boss will only keep you in one unit for a few months until it's humming like a top and you've taught someone else your job, and then he'll move you to another department."

(Within a month this person found a job that suited him perfectly and gave him the recognition he deserved. He later went on to become a corporate trainer of office managers, and a motivational speaker on the lecture circuit.)

Tip 71: Don't be afraid of hard work, as long as you love it

We spend a lot of time avoiding work that feels hard or unpleasant. Of course, there's nothing wrong with a good walk on the beach to relax, but if you find those intermissions are taking you away from what you want to be doing, one of two things may be going on: either you're putting your efforts in the wrong place – a signal that you haven't found the right form for your dream (see Tip 59) – or your inner Resistance is giving you reasons for not getting started.

Put your head down and pick up that work for a short time (promise yourself a nice break after 30 minutes of concentrated work). If you find that setting up some time limits makes the work more bearable, you're on the right track. If not, start asking yourself what changes you can make. You may have to go looking for a new form.

Tip 72: Protect yourself against risk (real and imaginary) as much as possible

People fear decision-making when it appears to be high risk. Therefore, it's important to design your search so the risks are low: don't invest a lot of money, don't burn any bridges, and don't sign any contracts.

Your hesitation to find what you love will probably melt if you remember you're merely deciding to investigate, to sample, to window-shop for your dream, not to sign up for anything or make any promises – or even any radical changes. And don't scare yourself to death with positive thinking, which has a way of creating imaginary risks: "I'm fantastic and I know I can do it!" may be very good when you're about to run a race, but it only makes you nervous over the long haul.

Trying to be perfect might be a reaction to the unfair rules of your childhood. Why create imaginary danger for the child inside you? Don't make big pronouncements. You don't have to be fantastic and you don't have to "know you can do it." You just have to decide to take the next step. That's how great things really get done.

Tip 73: Give yourself a chance to heal after a hard fall

If you've tried going after a dream and crashed, you should give yourself some time before trying again. Don't climb back on that horse right away. Your feelings need to heal before you can put your full weight on them, just like a broken bone.

Do a little bit in the direction of your dream each day, or simply think about it so it doesn't move too far back on the burner, but forgive yourself for not doing the most difficult parts for a while. You'll come back refreshed and ready to get into action. A broken bone, properly healed, is stronger than a bone that's never been broken at all.

Tip 74: Give yourself the right to dream

Some people don't know it's okay to start searching for what they love, like Angie. She didn't feel comfortable admitting her dream (working with tigers in the zoo) because it seemed utterly ridiculous. She wasn't even sure that was really her dream, since she'd never taken one step toward it. "Maybe I just saw a movie I liked, or something silly like that," she said. She forgot to take the very first step: giving herself the right to dream. She didn't even let herself fantasize about this secret wish because it was so far-fetched.

But you can't get anywhere if you're not at least willing to *pretend* that you're going after a dream. And pretending can give you the right to dream.

I told Angie to make a 5-year fantasy plan. That is, *if* she were going to move on the dream (not saying she actually *will*), what steps would she take to be sure she was doing it inside of 5 years? Just writing the steps down and gathering information, checking a web site and getting on a mailing list with people knowledgeable about working with tigers, helped her to realize she was supposed to be working toward her dream, not spending years preoccupied with finding something she didn't want.

Tip 75: Trust your feelings

Sometimes we try to make ourselves want something we really don't. But the problem is, you can't choose what you love. What you love chooses *you*. In fact, it's already chosen you, and now it's up to you to find it. Our gifts are with us from birth: we can't fashion them; we can only discover them.

Rule of thumb: When you're searching for what you love and you don't have a clue, the best way to start is by following your nose and trusting your feelings. If something looks like it should feel good but it doesn't, turn away until you find something that does.

Often we have to discover a new path with no guidelines, and neither reason nor experience nor advice can help us. The only way to find what you were designed to do is to trust your feelings. If you were standing at a table full of dozens of foods, you'd listen to your taste buds without a second thought. Choosing a dream is a lot like that.

Tip 76: When searching for an elusive dream, don't do two steps at once

First, you must allow yourself to dream without restrictions, like a child. *Then* you can subject your dream to reality, like an adult. If you try to do them both at the same time, you'll kill your dream just as it's peeking out of its hiding place, and it will disappear again.

Once your dream is visible and standing up in the sunlight, you can bring in all the reality you like. But if your dream never sees the light of day, you won't have that choice.

For example, don't fantasize and criticize at the same time or you'll never figure out what you love. First, fantasize something you'd love to do. Later, you'll decide how to do it, and that uses completely different tools. A writer doesn't write and edit at the same time. If you try to do two steps at the same time, you won't get anywhere.

Tip 77: Notice that goals are choices, but dreams are discoveries

To launch a serious search you must understand that you can't choose or build or design a dream, you can only discover it. Dreams start out in your biology: your dream is what you love and it's what you are designed to do. That's why it feels good when you do it. A goal, on the other hand, is chosen. You *can* invent it. And it's concrete and specific, with an outcome and a target date.

For example: "I've discovered that I'm only happy working outdoors, in nature," describes your dream. But you must also be willing to set a goal: "I want to experience at least 4 ways of working outdoors to find which one suits me best." That will create the actions you need to achieve your dream.

Incidentally, because you don't choose what you love, you don't have to defend it. If anyone says there's something wrong with what you want, just say, "I can't help it. That's the way it is."

Tip 78: Identify and rescue your secret mission by choosing a goal

Don't know what you want? Pick a 3-month goal based on something you care about. Don't demand that this goal has to be your dream – just that it isn't unimportant to you.

Now pursue it with every tool at your disposal: write a to-do list so you'll do the research, and talk to others who are knowledgeable about your goal (you'll find huge resources on the Internet. Head over to Google).

What's the point? You need a sense of direction, a feeling of forward movement. A short-term goal will grease your wheels and get you unstuck, and once that happens, you'll be free to go in any direction you choose. Most important, if you pick a goal that matters to you – and, if necessary, another one when this one is completed, and even another after that – you'll be closing in on your hidden mission, what it is you secretly feel you were put here to do. How?

You'll have experiences and encounter information you'd never have known about otherwise. You'll meet people with whom you have something in common. These can reveal a dream that was hidden only because you didn't know it existed!

Also, you'll start to see a common thread in all the goals you choose, and begin to identify the elements that appear in anything that's important to you. Draw a line through these commonalities and you'll see them point straight to your dream or at least in the right direction.

Tip 79: To get serious about finding your dream, think of an appealing outcome to your goal

To help you make the decision to pursue a dream using the method of pursuing a smaller goal (Tip 78), imagine an outcome that makes the effort worth your while. You'd be surprised how often we start working on a goal with a sense that the result will be pointless or disappointing.

While there's no point in hoping for an outcome that will disappoint you (I'll find exactly what I love and be filled with unutterable joy in 3 months!) you should be heading for something that will be interesting and satisfying to you.

For instance, "In three months I'll know more about what I want, I'll have learned things I never knew before, been places I never knew existed and have at least one new friend to talk with about my search."

Tip 80: Keep your eye on the outcome and you'll find a way to get there

You can't swim the English Channel unless you know France is there on the other side. You can't sing a high C unless you hear it first in your mind. Watch a dog jump up into a car: he pins his eyes on where he wants to be, gathers his body into a spring and shoots right up to it. Without a destination, it's hard to find motivation.

There are other ways of finding what you love (follow your nose and only choose what makes you happy, for one) but if motivation is a problem, you need a goal. Don't worry about choosing the wrong goal. Just make it something you'd like to accomplish that's not too far off. Once you get there, you can decide where you want to go next.

Tip 81: Set performance goals to keep yourself moving

Did you give it your best shot? That's all that matters with performance goals. Performance goals aren't about where you're going but about how much effort you're putting into the journey. They'll keep you moving, even if your outcome goal sometimes seems impossible to find.

Here's an example of some performance goals: "My goal is to do all the exercises in Barbara's books," "My goal is to make 12 calls this week to try to get information," "My goal is to start working on this project every day at noon."

Tip 82: Be willing to accept your discoveries about what you need

You can't get serious about searching for a goal unless you make it your only duty to discover what your deepest needs are. Do you want to find some kind of work you'll love to do every day, or is that less important than a general kind of lifestyle?

"I have to live in a beautiful place and have a job where I work with a good team of people," said a client recently. "If I have those two things, I don't really care what I'm doing all day." That's what I call a lifestyle wish.

Another said, "I have to be a dancer. That's what really matters to me." This isn't a lifestyle desire; it's the desire to do a special, beloved kind of "work," in this case to dance. Take note of where your desire lies.

Tip 83: Say yes to every low-risk, new experience that interests you

Nothing has the power to teach like experience and no experience is wasted. The moment something interests you, even a little, make a firm commitment to find out more about it.

You don't need a good excuse to sign up for a one-time class in solar energy when you live in a big city and have no possible way to use that information. If you're intrigued, trust that there's a good reason for it and follow your impulse. You may not understand what use it will be, but when you pursue things that intrigue you, you're making a directed search without knowing it.

One day these experiences will turn out to be exactly what you needed to do exactly what you love.

Tip 84: Don't get locked in thought: Go exploring

Beware of what a client of mine called "analysis paralysis." Nothing will guide you like actual information and there's no way to get that sitting alone examining options and risks for the nth time. Sometimes, like an inventor, a research scientist, or an explorer, you have to pick yourself up and move toward whatever makes you curious.

Exploration does not equal commitment, so you don't need to analyze your move to death. Action will give you more fresh information than any amount of analysis. You can speculate all you like about what you should be doing with your life, but until you visit a real scene you won't know for sure. Action will allow you to realize you don't like certain things so can forget them. It also lets you know right away when you love something.

If you need to give an excuse, just call it "research."

Tip 85: Claim your freedom to make mistakes

Anyone who believes you shouldn't make mistakes doesn't have their head on right. There's simply no other way to learn. Just don't makes the stakes too high – so if you're wrong, you can still play again.

Should you worry about your family's values or take a stand on something that matters to you? What if you turn out to be wrong? You can only be wrong if you made your choice out of rebellion. A rebellion against what your family wants will give you the exact opposite of it, not what you really want at all. Rebellion eats your freedom as much as giving in completely.

Set your goals without reference to anything but what's inside you. Remember, dreams are messages sent by your talent, and talent isn't social, it's biological. It's part of your genes, not your family's values. You have to set a goal as if no one were watching or would ever know about it. When you do that, you'll understand what freedom really is.

And what if you fail? Freedom includes the freedom to try until you get it right, no matter how many mistakes you make. If you feel you've *got* to be right or you've *got* to be a success, it's time for you to get your freedom back.

Tip 86: Let yourself be foolish once every week

Choosing action will give you courage and integrity, but most of us would rather die than be seen as foolish in public. The time has come to change that.

Decide today that you're going to allow yourself to be wildly embarrassed at least once every week. Pay yourself for it, if you like. Put money into an account that will get you a great vacation or some object you really love, because warriors should be rewarded.

Momentary emotional safety at the cost of many hours of sorrow and regret always reveals itself as a bad bargain.

Should you risk embarrassment and rejection by going after something you want, or remain safely in the shadows? What will you feel if you take these kinds of emotional chances? Well, you might feel foolish, or like a big jerk. It's possible and there's no point pretending otherwise.

Now weigh those feelings against the satisfaction of doing what you love every day, something you truly believe in.

Weigh the safety of not acting against the joy of moving ahead in your life, finding something or someone you love and getting what you need to create a great life.

Tip 87: Sum it up at night

How did today go? Notice what you did well so the accomplishment won't slip away – then you can remember it before it sinks below the foam of all the other things on your mind. If a horse wins a race, they notice it for a long time. If you win one, it's only good 'til lunchtime.

Let's change that, because you win a lot of races every day and forget to take notice. That's like throwing your change in the wastebasket when you empty your pockets at night. Just remember your achievements, and they'll go in the bank and make you feel a sense of plenty.

What about lessons you must learn? You'll notice as you go through your day that you're dissatisfied with your performance here and there. Shouldn't you "resolve to do better"? Absolutely not. Let it go. You'll change automatically, just by noting it.

Tip 88: Remember, asking for help is not a sign of incompetence or weakness

Let's just put an end to that myth right now. I'm talking about the lone hero, braving it on his own and (against all odds) realizing his vision, which no one else understands until he succeeds.

That story might give you a great feeling while you're watching a movie, but it's a recipe for disaster when going after a dream. I don't care how many talk show guests describe how they've made it on their own; everyone needs help and if you don't ask for it when you come up against an obstacle, you and your dream will get stuck for no good reason.

Start making a habit of asking for help – in the form of information, or paid assistance or just some company while you work on something difficult – even when it's not absolutely necessary. You'll be amazed at the amount of creative energy you get when you don't have to do everything yourself.

Asking for help doesn't mean you're helpless: it means that you care more about your dream than your ego.

Tip 89: Just because you have no idea how to do something doesn't mean you shouldn't do it

I'll say it again: dreams are messages sent to you from your talent, and they must be answered. If you have a dream of producing Rap records but don't know the first thing about sound equipment (or Rap!), who says you can't learn? What you love has nothing to do with the skills or knowledge you've acquired until now, but it has everything to do with where your gifts lie.

If you have the desire to try out something you know nothing about, make it your first goal to find out where you can learn more. Start at your local bookstore or on the Internet. Take a one-day class on the subject at one of the adult learning centers in your area. If you're still interested, make it your next goal to find out how to get some hands-on experience. If it turns out to be something you really love, you'll waste no time learning everything there is to know.

Soon, you'll be wondering what took you so long to get started.

Tip 90: Remember, a dream doesn't have to make money in order to "count"

Use your own standards to measure your dream, not someone's standards that don't apply. Most of the greatest dreams in history didn't make money and weren't intended to (like those of Dr. Schweitzer in Africa, Joan of Arc, Albert Einstein, Dr. Martin Luther King, Jr.)

Your goal might be to have more fun in your life, or to travel more, or to dedicate yourself to saving children around the world or saving the environment, or to paint again. Whatever it may be, check it to make sure it's what you'll *love* doing and leave out all other considerations.

Remember: Love is the only validation your dream needs – and it's the only element that will guarantee success.

Tip 91: Put a fair value on what you already do

Once you declare your freedom to go after what you love, there's sometimes a tendency to scorn what you do now, whether it's staying at home and raising children or punching stuff into a computer. That's a mistake for two reasons: First, any work you do is an accomplishment that deserves respect, yours above all. Take pride in the hard work you do to keep things running smoothly for yourself and your family. Add in the fact that it may not be your dream job, and I'd say you deserve a medal.

Second, that sense of pride is going to take you very far when going after what you really love. Use it as an asset in finding your dream and making it real. If you've come this far doing something that didn't make you jump for joy, just imagine how great you'll be at what you were truly designed to do!

Tip 92: Memorize the feeling of freedom

Life gets complicated when your obligations pull you in many different directions at once. As you give yourself the freedom to go after your dreams, you may feel these obligations start to weigh you down. They may not even be real, just leftover feelings of guilt and anxiety about doing what you love.

Before you start to panic that your dream won't be able to survive, stop right now and take a deep breath. Things aren't all that complicated. You really only need one important thing to simplify your life: a memory of the feeling of freedom you've attained – that is free time, freedom from guilt and worry, freedom from having to defend your decisions. Just imagine it.

You see, if you cut back on your obligations you'll give yourself some time to do what you love, and that's great. But until the sense of freedom gets hardwired in your mind, you won't be able to use it right, and soon you'll just fill it up again with more obligations.

We're all prisoners of what we think we should do. Going after your dreams is the key to freedom; and it's yours to use when you need it.

Tip 93: If you're not sure where to start, make a plan; it doesn't even have to be a good one

A plan isn't a machine. It's a prediction, a way of thinking about a project, a wish. "Why bother? I've made so many plans of action that didn't yield a thing. They could fill a book!" one client told me. But the problem wasn't with the plan or her lack of resolve. She was just putting the emphasis in the wrong place. A plan isn't supposed to be a contract you make to achieve some goal: it's to get you thinking about good ways to get there. And that's valuable information you *do* need.

Make a plan that includes some concrete steps in the direction of your dream. Even if you take just one step and realize you need a new plan, you'll know more than when you started. Plans themselves don't always make things happen, but they're a great way to get you off your couch and out where happy accidents do.

Tip 94: Accept setbacks

Prepare yourself to be sidelined now and then by things completely out of your control. Someone might cancel an interview or forget to send a check or change their mind at the last minute. You might get hit by a flood or the flu.

There's no way to prevent these things, so you just have to accept that they do happen – and that they aren't permanent. Your plans will get back on track soon enough if you're ready for the setbacks. If you're not, it can take a lot longer to get over your feelings of pain and disappointment.

Remember: Setbacks are part of the process. Something interesting often comes from them.

Epilogue

I hope you've enjoyed this collection of essential tips and words of wisdom. Time and again, I've watched people's dreams go from "utterly impossible" to "totally doable" within minutes, just by showing them there's always a way to do what you love – if you're willing to dump some old assumptions and make finding your dreams a top priority.

Everything you've just read was put there with that goal in mind. Because nothing in this life is more important than realizing your gifts and sharing them with the world. And nothing makes me happier than believing you are about to do just that.

I'd love to hear from you. If you'd like to share your thoughts and any stories about finding your dreams, please feel free to write me at bsherny@earthlink.net.

You should also come to exchange ideas, experiences, problems and advice with me and thousands of other smart, supportive dreamfinders in my very special online community. See the list of links on the next page for the places on the Internet where you can find and connect with us. Let's all help each other achieve our dreams!

I'm very pleased you took the time to read these pages and are giving your dreams and gifts the attention they deserve. I look forward to hearing about all the wonderful things you're going to accomplish.

Sincerely,

Barbara

Barbara Sher on the Internet

Barbara's Club – barbarasclub.com

Original website – barbarasher.com

Bulletin boards – boards.barbarasher.com

Facebook page – www.facebook.com/BarbaraSherAuthor

Twitter – @BarbaraSher – twitter.com/BarbaraSher

LinkedIn – www.linkedin.com/in/barbarasher

YouTube - www.youtube.com/user/WriteSpeaker/videos

Pinterest – www.pinterest.com/TheBarbaraSher

Instagram – www.instagram.com/sherbarbara

TEDxPrague 2015 – https://youtu.be/H2rG4Dg6xyI

Publisher of this book – www.beyond-mountains.com

Books by Barbara Sher

Wishcraft: How to Get What You Really Want, (1979)

Teamworks: Building Support Groups That Guarantee Success (1989)

I Could Do Anything if I Only Knew What It Was: How to Discover What You Really Want and How to Get It (1994)

Live the Life You Love: In 10 Easy Step-By-Step Lessons (1996)

It's Only Too Late If You Don't Start Now: How to Create Your Second Life At Any Age (1999)

Refuse to Choose!: Use All of Your Interests, Passions, and Hobbies to Create the Life and Career of Your Dreams (2006)

What Do I Do When I Want to Do Everything?: A Revolutionary Programme for Doing Everything That You Love (2006) - UK edition of Refuse to Choose

Printed in Great Britain
by Amazon

84417989R00089